# kigo
# 季語

FOUR SEASONS IN HAIKU

DANIEL MEDINA

Edited by Flor Ana Mireles

1st Edition | 01
Paperback ISBN: 979-8-9862106-5-0

First Published September 2023

For inquiries and bulk orders, please email:
indieearthpublishinghouse@gmail.com

Printed in the United States

1 2 3 4 5 6 7 8 9

Indie Earth Publishing Inc.
| Miami, FL |

# kigo 季語

## FOUR SEASONS IN HAIKU

DANIEL MEDINA

# Contents

# kigo 季語

## FOUR SEASONS IN HAIKU

DANIEL MEDINA

*"Spring passes and one remembers one's innocence. Summer passes and one remembers one's exuberance. Autumn passes and one remembers one's reverence. Winter passes and one remembers one's perseverance."*

— Yoko Ono

To my parents, Daniel E. Medina y Maria T. Medina, words do not contain or can genuinely express my love, admiration, and respect for both of you. *Infinitissimas gracias por su amor y ejemplos intachables.*

*– Su hijo, Daniel*

And to every sincere seeker of truth walking upon this Earth authentically desiring to see and touch the face of God.

# KIGO
## A Preface to the Seasons

Four seasons. There are four reasons for why I selected the structure of a year to express a life in process—still unfolding, at times blossoming, evolving, and understanding the reason for being—while embracing mystery, learning to feel comfortable in ambiguity, realizing that my truth is as sure as anything I'll ever be, and that faith is not about having the answers but learning to live with the questions.

And it was these life experiences, events, and, for lack of a better word, seasons—my childhood, adolescence, and early youth—that helped me define my sense of identity, my understanding of what the meaning of my life is, and to identify the questions that are the most salient, difficult, and valuable to me as a human being and artist. It is through these two sources of "being" that I define myself and comprehend what I need to be and do while on this planet, on the side of "living," as it were.

I have always been told that I feel "too much." I grew into a person who struggled with being that way, and yet, I couldn't ever stop myself. I was also identified as a "dreamer" and "free spirit," and these labels were not tooted and shared; I kept them within as a "responsible" individual, especially a male, needing to be both comported and formalized.

Yet, the magical world of seasons and the daily interplay of my five senses with the world of matter around me instigated deeper questions about why, who, when, how, and where... I didn't simply accept things as they were; there had to be more and a deeper cause, effect, and purpose—a meaning that either wasn't shared, or most didn't want to know.

The church seasons made so much sense to me. The lives of the saints and the equinoxes and solstices, in essence, spoke to me. Dusks, dawns, twilights, and those stars! My goodness, the constellations—and over the months, they changed protagonists on this eternal tapestry above the electric lights of the city and the occasional ones flickering inside my home. Snow, forests, rain, the open sea, storms, the desert, and the endless sense of space under the desert night sky are indiscernible; they point toward a deeper mystery of cycles, changes, and rhythms. As I studied music, later painting, and world religions, I began to trace these beautiful patterns across all peoples, languages, and systems of beliefs; indeed, as President Kennedy once said, "we all breathe the same air."

But it's even more than all this—these encounters with a sense of soul and place beyond myself were grounded forevermore in my life when I read the works of Ralph Waldo Emerson, especially *The*

*Oversoul, Spiritual Laws, and Circles*. In these writings, as in those of the great faith traditions of the East and West, and in the novels and poetry of Jack Kerouac, I found *The Scripture of the Golden Eternity* was, in fact, manifested by Autumn's celestial railroad across countless miles painted in orange, brown, red, and yellow, in the palpable wonder I felt at smelling smoke from wood-burning chimneys on chilly Winter evenings, in the smell of rain and the cool drops of South Florida showers throughout Spring, and in the intense embrace of the Summer sun.

The four seasons are the four corners of my world, the cardinal points of my truest sense of existence, and the pillars that sustain and support the ideas, thoughts, worldview, beliefs, and perspectives in the mind that make me who I am. To forget them is to lose myself.

I chose to memorialize my life in Haiku because the details of my stories are personal, for family and the closest of friends. I am certain that as I age further, those no longer here will come closer to me, and the meaning of those events will grow in even greater significance to me and to those I am blessed to counsel and care for. American Haiku Pop was the term coined by Jack Kerouac to identify and point in the direction of the jazz poetry he was writing (and creating).

Just like Allen Ginsburg, Kerouac believed the details of the traditional Japanese poetics called Haiku would require a different headspace and approach as Westerners and as being from a culture so radically different than the one that birthed Haiku. Like Jazz, American Haiku Pop provides the poet with a loose structure and form of Haiku while allowing the poet to improvise and reconfigure the poetics to reflect the life lived rather than seeking to emulate another's structure, which is structured so differently due to religion, culture, and above all else, language.

I do not claim to be an expert or to have ever achieved the greatness of Richard Wright, Jack Kerouac, Allen Ginsburg, or innumerable other poets. But in the end, like a jazz musician, I count off, follow the charts, groove to the spirit, and share with you, my readers, my truth, veiled in language, disguised in mystery, and making the space within the song for you to venture into your imagination and see yourself in these poems. This is what art is: a mirror held before us so that we can reencounter and re-commune with our better angels.

*Daniel Medina*
*August 10, 2023*
*The Feast Day of Saint Lawrence of Rome*
*Little Havana, FL*

KIGO

# WINTER

*"Melancholy were the sounds on a winter's night."*
*— Virginia Woolf*

## Introduction to the original preface

**D**uring the first Winter of the global COVID-19 pandemic, I decided to memorialize the four seasons in an annual haiku book of days.

As I reflect on contents therein, I am struck by how I am transported to that time—visceral—with the trepidation, and if I confess, a sense of wonder of what was unfolding before the entire human population all at once. I am also taken aback by the abysmal wedge still prevalent among family, friends, colleagues, and neighbors over all sorts of political and social differences in our country.

Not much has changed, while much has. I've had the opportunity to travel around the sun three more times since the original preface was written. And yet, I find myself to be a different person—with a vantage point some would refer to as incomprehensible while others would simply say, "He's a dreamer, he's always been." I believe in the undying capacity within most human beings to reconnect with their better angels. That's what art is there for.

Even amongst the artists who feel absolutely no need or responsibility to engage the existential challenges of the human condition, they do—it's inevitable. For whether intended or not, art doesn't ask permission from the parents who conceived it to go this way or that. Once able to be free from the constraints and helicopter oversight of the artist, the work arrives at the shores of new hearts, minds, and experiences. As in traditions of some faiths, one's return to heaven will be accompanied with a new name, a new title.

So it is with art.

*Daniel Medina*
*July 23, 2023*
*Feast Day of St. Bridget of Sweden*
*Miami, FL*

## Preface

Winter is a remarkable time.

It is a season of light as well as darkness. A time when spirits seem to be enlivened and challenged by the sense of time passing, light diminishing, and another year about to end. Winter invokes memories.

As a child, Winter represented everything to me that was mysterious about my religious faith. Winter also unveiled the mystery of nature. I was sensitive to the changes in the weather. My mother and I would sit on our porch and exchange smiles that revealed the knowledge of Winter's imminent arrival, as if we were adepts of an esoteric cabal.

After Thanksgiving, Winter's coming was all fanfare—at least in Miami, where Winter is mild in comparison to Chicago, the city where some of my most vivid childhood Christmas memories still transport me to the two-story, bungalow-style family home on North Ashland Avenue in Andersonville.

As I grew, Winter was also associated with my struggles and with people now gone. Some of my most important gigs as a musician occurred in Winter. Some of the most difficult experiences in my life, as a soldier, as a man, as a son, and later, as a father, happened in Winter.

I selected Winter as the first book in my Year in Haiku Project because it marks the end of the previous year and is the arena where we are all ushered into the new as one human race. Not one of us can skip Winter or choose to have anything to do with such a challenging season.

When COVID-19 appeared on the world stage, one early idea to foster hope and offer encouragement was to decorate homes with Christmas lights. It was also a concern that colder temperatures could exacerbate the pandemic's already deadly spread. Such a dichotomy. Contrasts—like night and day, light and darkness, joy, and sorrow—make the most wonderful time of the year, and for innumerable of our neighbors, the loneliest.

Winter is the time we are told to proclaim peace on Earth. It is when goodwill toward humankind is celebrated, sung about, preached about, and hoped for. Yet, this Winter, on January 6, 2021, the total and unadulterated antithesis of these proclamations took place on Capitol Hill.

Perhaps this Winter of discontent will be transformed into a glorious summer. I believe we all can aspire to see our better angels rise to the surface as new blooms in the spring, but it cannot occur unless we are willing to let the old ways fall like autumn leaves.

I pray these poems are a service in this process. Reflection can be a powerful exercise, but only if accompanied by actions that demonstrate wisdom, empathy, and humility.

I have lived through fifty-one winters. These are the poems that memorialize my life during that season.

It is an honor to share them with you.

*Daniel Medina*
*January 7, 2021*
*Orthodox Christmas Day*
*Miami, FL*

# WINTER

## Reflections & Remembrances

Each log burns, hoping
Although you're close, you're so far
Time burns hope away

Christmas trees thrown out
The times are disposable
Tempted to take home

Cold air swept through town
That corner house reminds me
Baptize *el lechón*

Planets united
While humans kept their distance
On a midnight clear

*Winter*

New year and false starts
Resolutions indict all
Change is not instant

*Winter*

The season is here
As a child, I loved it
Leave it behind soon

Evenings are crisp now
Memories are warm and old
They are not kind

Music elevates
The spirit yearns for meaning
Improvise the hope

O SMOKING
GO TO
JAIL
MARVIN GARDENS
$280
WATER WORKS
$150
VENTNOR AVENUE
$260
$200

Peace on Earth has come
Goodwill has left the planet
No room left for Love

Where has the time gone
Stories don't resemble mine
Not in the mood now

I recall the days
Cold
Painting
expecting you
Seems like years ago

Stars conspire
The complacency of hearts
The end of routine

I remember snow
Mesmerized by tree lights
The large porch was home

Loneliness calls home
Time is difficult to face
"Then" doesn't return

Cold morning again
Another warm afternoon
Bundle up with shorts

God made flesh
The season to be jolly
The man of sorrows

Familiar with pain
The cold does warm my heart though
Rationalizing

Past *Noche Buenas*
The evening was magical
All is quiet now

I played Herod once
I excelled as a shepherd
Dad was a Magi

Shepherds and churros
Angels with garland halos
Drank chocolate too

Bloodshed on the Hill
A tyrant's words lead to death
Epiphany Day

Memories are seared
Fire embraces to burn
He makes all things new

Nativity plays
Los Sobrinos del Juez sing
Hialeah lights

Snow covered the streets
Comic-shopping, just us three
I can't take his calls

A tree is dormant
Old Man Winter bids farewell
The Green Man cometh

# SPRING

*"On soft Spring nights I'll stand in the yard under the stars - Something good will come out of all things yet - And it will be golden and eternal just like that - There's no need to say another word."*
*— Jack Kerouac*

## Introduction to the original preface

It is one of the hottest summers in recorded history on planet Earth. In Miami, where I reside, it is 102 degrees Fahrenheit. It is a good day to think of Spring. Not a Miami Spring, by the way—a northern one.

As I reread the preface, I am struck by the intense experiences Spring provided for me as a boy and later as a young man. If I am honest, I struggled through Spring. I didn't feel I blossomed sufficiently and was usually caught off guard by the beach days (I was very self-conscious) and by the need to get out there and beyond my introverted self.

I usually looked and stayed within myself, never a social butterfly—a classic Spring insect. Instead, I am the type to focus on the how the butterfly is ancient symbol of resurrection, and I'd prefer to share that with someone that actually dug that rather than to be going from one person to the next at some gathering.

Spring was (and is becoming more) of a time of reflection for me. As Spring carries over the remnant of the Yuletide season—in the sense of the stories that significantly influence my life as a writer and artist in general—I see the time of preparation, similar to that of Advent in the Autumn and into the early Winter season as that: reflection, inner work, and coming to sincere terms with what keeps me from growing and bearing fruit, as it were, blossoming. These are not trite questions; they may seem to be for the vocabulary can be jaded for many.

Be that as it may, the sense of growth I came to understand as I think of the 53 Springs I have been able to enjoy tells me that we come out of the confines of frosted circumstances—almost as if are coming out of deep paralyzing sleep—to face the opportunity for new things to fill the void left behind by the things that remained lifeless over the course of the last year. And many things do.

I have written that seasons can leave ambiguous consequences or experiences for us. I stand by that more than ever before. What may have at an earlier stage in life seemed to be such a terrible outcome, one later rejoices to see how the outcomes were a blessings in disguised.

I had to learn to be an extrovert. I had to learn to let others see my fruits and blossoms of my mind and heart, and to that end, be able to stand before others with the confidence I often shrugged aside as not being for me to enjoy or impossible for me to ever feel comfortable in having.

These poems attest to those struggles and the longing I harbor for those people, occasions, places, and life. I believe art stands in the gap of the space left behind by the past and leads the artist as a lamp toward an undetermined future. Haiku allows for the reader to go beyond the façade afforded by the poet so the reader can embrace and evaluate a life lived and entertain and enjoin oneself to a new life tomorrow.

*Daniel Medina*
*July 23, 2023*
*Feast Day of St. Bridget of Sweden*
*Miami, FL*

## Preface

Spring.

As a boy at Kensington Park Elementary School, I sat in an old fashioned desk in the back of the classroom. It was my music/choir class. We'd sing as a class from 1950s singing books. I loved them. I loved how each song was illustrated, along with providing the lyrics and musical arrangement. Somehow, the book would transport me to another place. It was a good place.

There was a particular song I still find myself occasionally humming. Although I haven't been able to find the book or song ever again, its beautiful and haunting melody still ushers Spring for me—almost half a century later.

In terms of weather, Spring was not very cool in Miami, Florida. It often felt as pre-Summer than anything else. Humidity, mosquitoes, and rain by May—if not earlier. However, the evenings provided immaculate sunsets, and there was a refreshing drop in temperature every so often.

As a child, Easter was the centerpiece of the season. Passion plays and church (sacred) cantatas were the events I looked forward to as many of my childhood friends participated, and rehearsals were hilarious and unforgettable. These memorable experiences were juxtaposed to the ending of school. In many ways, late Spring represented a time of tension and one of peace. One of reflection and introspection as I approached Summer and knew things would never be the same.

In my late teens, my dad had this tradition he wanted all of us to join in on—and we did, but not for the reasons he intended. The Diplomat Hotel on Miami Beach was considered one of the top resorts for South Florida tourists and residents for many decades. It still is. Every Memorial Day weekend, my dad would reserve a room for the national holiday, but… we knew that as soon as my dad would pick up our keys, we'd take the elevator, and the old man put the key into the doorknob, it would start to rain and not stop until we checked out.

Over the weekend, as we sat in the lobby looking out into Noah's deluge, my dad would stand in front of the huge, 15-foot glass wall of the beautiful and immense hotel lobby generously decorated with chandeliers and paintings on the high cathedral ceilings, which the likes of Frank Sinatra, Liza Minnelli, Mohammad Ali, Sammy Davis, Jr., Mel Brooks, Ronald Reagan, Bill Clinton, and Dean Martin enjoyed. My father would stoically stand with his arms behind him and nod to the right and the left, saying colorful, Cuban obscenities to himself with such nimble acumen that unstoppable tears would pour out as we tried for dear life to hold back the laughter. He somehow thought he should've known it would rain—again.

These were some of the most memorable experiences of past Springs in my life. A time of transition and anticipation. As I grow older, Spring has taken on a more significant place in my life. As a teacher, it's the final stretch for my students. As a minister, it's a time of death and resurrection. I took many trips with my parents around this season, and the floods of memories are quite overwhelming at times, to be quite honest. As a father, the joy of making Easter eggs and egg hunts will always remain as vibrant recollections to me. Bunnies and Crosses.

Over time, many societies and civilizations have understood Spring as a time of rebirth, rejuvenation, awakening, and growth. Health and blossoms, warmer temperatures and the ushering into the radiant heat and potential of Summer is Spring's irreplaceable role in this planet's life cycle and in the human relationships with God, Nature, and one another. This collection of poems attempts to provide my subjective insights into all three.

As I have written before, Haiku is irreplaceable to me. It offers the unique opportunity to share my most intimate and priceless moments with each of you without revealing the details to anyone. There is a sublime lesson to this. Like Spring, the Source of Life that enables and afforded me with the privileges to experience the moments of joy, love, pain, uncertainty, fear, loss, celebration, and hope, I record in this collection are the impressions of my life navigating through them. You will see yourself in these words. You may discover lost feelings, restore forgotten memories, and reawaken to this Spring with vigor and hopeful anticipation. Perhaps the experience will be difficult and, at times, unwanted.

Seasons have power over us. Seasons possess this potent characteristic because we are inextricably connected to them. Our lives aren't as linear as some science suggests and philosophies argue. Spring affords all of us a chance to renew commitments to ourselves. Spring offers an opportunity to restart our lives and pursue those things that provide life, not just for a season,but for as long as we have on the Earth to do so.

May the poems stimulate the thoughts that free you from yesterday, embrace the lessons they may have for you, let go of what is not possible to change, and see yourself as genuinely able (and deserving) to bear new blossoms, fruits, and bask in the light you may have avoided before.

*Daniel Medina*
*Candlemas*
*February 2, 2021*
*Miami, FL*

# SPRING

## Intimations & Improvisations

On April 15th
Snow upon snow was magic
Unlike Miami

# *Spring*

Two weeks for Winter
Just one week for Spring
How sad
The line fantastic

I played Herod once
Now
I am playing Satan
Rave reviews
                    I'm dead

I wore my A's top
Seven was our number, too
Medina Seven

I saw Him walking
He was bleeding and beaten
Undeniable

Spring is life and death
Loss of life seems distant now
Egg hunts and beaches

With flying colors
Heading down Brickell
Mami was waiting

Fools and innocents
Bunnies and baskets
Showers and flowers

Thinking about Spring
And how it changed my life
A time of repose

This year I will change
Making right so much on hold
Settling no more

Stars conspired then
And stars will never cease to
Their light reminds us

Valentine flies by
Easter comes and goes as quick
All ephemeral

Spring is somewhat strange
Birth and death embrace somehow
Sublime oracle

The Black Destiny
We wore Z. Cavaricci
Club Clue Non-Stop, bro

Playing *The Reflex*
Off to Hojo's to see Rick
Unforgettable

Memories are clear
When will they begin to fade?
Hesse's *Long Summer*

Fire embers glow
The ground trembles with new life
Now desensitized

Maypoles delight me
I garden to be closer
Mornings at the beach

The year is still new
The year is simmering, too
Soon we shall harvest

May for Pumpkin Seeds
Christmas Trees in March
Time slows down for youth

Regrets like bedbugs
Spiritual hobos travel
Birdsongs in the rain

In March I lost her
His birthday was on May 7th
Brutal New Year's Eve

Flowers in mid-March
Lilies on Easter Sunday
Gladiolus for them

On St. Brigid's Day
Ahead of the Equinox
How's the weather?

Sun cracks through the blinds
Now light shines through broken hearts
Life begins with light

Graduation thoughts
Another time was lived then
Summer is here soon

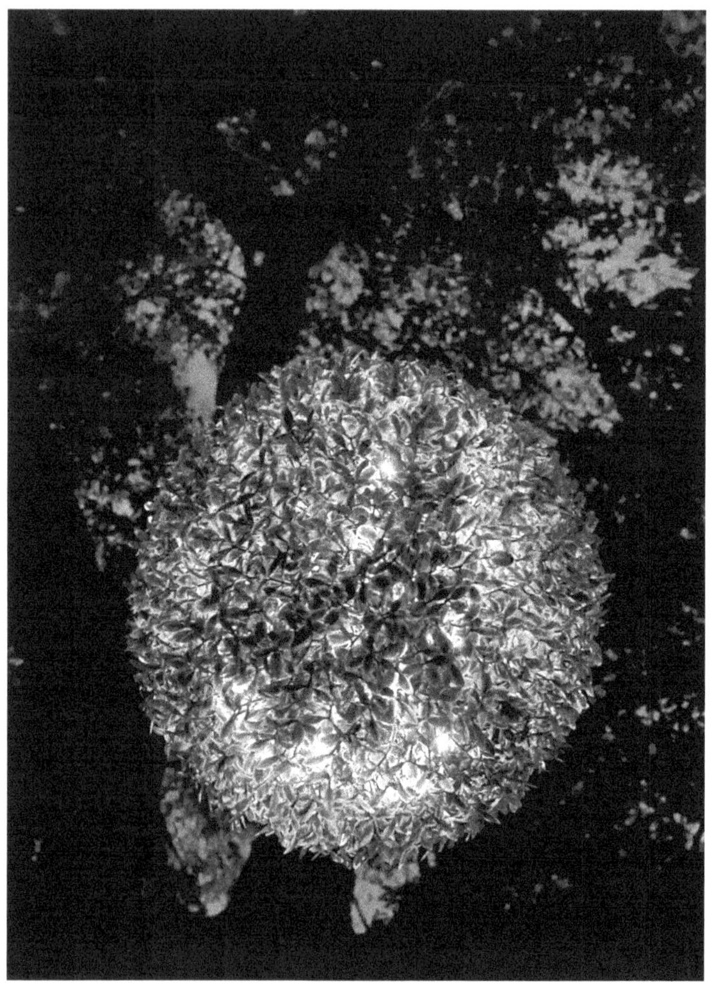

# SUMMER

*"The summer ended. Day by day, and taking its time, the summer ended. The noises in the street began to change, diminish, voices became fewer, the music sparse. Daily, blocks and blocks of children were spirited away. Grownups retreated from the streets, into the houses. Adolescents moved from the sidewalk to the stoop to the hallway to the stairs, and rooftops were abandoned. Such trees as there were allowed their leaves to fall - they fell unnoticed - seeming to promise, not without bitterness, to endure another year..."*

*— James Baldwin*

## Introduction to the original preface

The nature of following the four seasons through Haiku was an effort to review many dimensions of my life and provide a frame within which to memorialize them with vulnerability and authenticity. Poetry has afforded me the language and structure I need to do that.

Much of my life has been spent taking the images that remain after whatever experience I had and enhancing them with sound, as in the sound of a voice or a statement made. I would add a soundtrack to it as well. My childhood friend and I would also make ridiculous storylines about our experiences and make the characters in them come to life by taking on similar aspects of TV and film protagonists or villains we enjoyed.

Needless to say, the memories of those days make up for so many of those ambiguous occurrences we happen to undergo and the ones we don't want to, but yet have to somehow and in some way.

It was during my youthful Summers that I acquired a knack for humor. I'd say I discovered the natural inclination or predisposition I possessed for converting a potentially uncomfortable situation into one in which laughter could be introduced and enjoyed. I discovered that this disarmed others and diffused many uncomfortable moments. Was it a means of escape? Perhaps.

I found Summer to be an escape from the drudgery of school and, early on, from the bullying I experienced and the need to endure the daily monotony of school structures and expectations. By the time high school rolled around, I had discovered art and music, particularly, and was able to deal with much of my angst and uncertainties through the channeling afforded to me by sounds, lyrics, melodies, and harmonies. I am eternally grateful for music. I believe it saved my life through God's grace, to be sure.

Then , travel became an essential part of my being. After reading Jack Kerouac's seminal novel, On The Road, I decided to do the same with my trusty 1977 Chevrolet Capric Classic, christened "*DAS BOOT*" by my close friend group. As immortalized by the lyrics of Love Shack by the B-52: "I got me a car, it's as big as a whale... I got me a Chrysler, it seats about twenty—So hurry up and bring your jukebox money![1]" the car was immense. With art, travel, and my upbringing instilled in me—as I wrote in the original preface, "an incessant pursuit of deeper, spiritual grounding"—I see Haiku as an avenue for plumbing my subjective understanding of these matters, and now I can share them with you. May they be of since-

1 *Songwriters: Cindy Wilson / Fred Schneider / Kate Pierson / Keith Strickland Love Shack lyrics © Kobalt Music Publishing Ltd., Sony/ATV Music Publishing LLC*

re service in unlocking your potential and a catalyst to go on the road in mind, body, and soul.

*Daniel Medina*
*July 25, 2023*
*Christmas in July*
*Little Havana, FL*

## Preface

Summer has always been highly welcomed by me. I had a peculiar fear of school—I'd say almost a phobia— and Summer afforded me emotional shelter, fun, and opportunities to recuperate and bond with myself, my family, and the greater world. I found solace in Summer and awaited each day with joyful anticipation.

For several years, Summer represented deep, painful loss. It seems I am reliving those rain-drenched days as I write these words. As in the case of Christmas, Summer was once innocent, and as far as I knew, there wasn't anything that could take their innocence away from me.

I was wrong.

Summer represents an important aspect of my youth and my life in general. I used to spend Summers in Chicago. Those were magical times unlike anything else I had experienced. I traveled to Europe, South America, and the Caribbean as a boy and young man. Summers then took me to further and more exotic locations around the world. Summer represents a time to travel for the inner life and for the discovery of manifold points of connection between us and our beloved planet.

As I anticipated these poems to take on flesh and a life of their own, I wasn't careless in recognizing the peculiar sense of rhythm between youthful remembrance and an incessant pursuit of deeper, spiritual grounding. These two experiences were concordant and walked hand in hand as Summers past and I anticipated another season in the vibrant sun. I pray these Haiku are in some way able to generate the thoughts, reflections, and inner conversations that will help you heal, grow, and enjoy your life. If the conditions are less than ideal, may this book serve as a companion toward your liberation. If you are in a season of plenty, may this book grant you much delight.

*Daniel Medina*
*July 11, 2021*
*Feast of St. Benedict*
*Little Havana, FL*

# SUMMER

## Muses & Meditations

Summer on Sunset
Vintage Bakery Centre
Boyz With Da New Look

Walking to Bird Road
Refreshing Big Gulps to boot!
Shadows in the rain

Wet serpentine roads
Light radiates through fresh leaves
Fresh coffee in hand

The last day of school
All students yelled, "Hail, Caesar!"
"Captain, my Captain!"

My boss Vasano
Went to see the Pope, no joke
Next year in Cuba

Waves that ebb and flow
Are like the days long ago
And part of the One

Fire pits in Summer
Another kind of fire
Crackling purifies

There is one building
Across from a gorgeous church
It knows my life well

August in London
Lime gelato in Capri
Transformational

Summer backyard games
Imagination ran wild
Here is where I write

Christmas in July
An effort never realized
Seems artificial

Twenty-two Summers
My life was born on the 10th
July is witness

Stars conspiring now
I believe dreams never fade
Sanding hourglass

Follow your own way
Every grain of sand affords
Grace abounds for all

*Summer*

Summer vibrancy
Roads are traveled—limitless
Life's catch and release

Fifty-one Summers
From mountains and deserts seen
Life's rich pageant there

On Biltmore's grass lay
The fireworks of freedom
A magical night

Across Lincoln Square
Central Park's Strawberry Fields
God prepared that night

Long roadtrips with you
We never saw trips the same
To live that again

The fragrance of wood
As it burns so I can dream
Selfless-love perfumed

Anticipating time
Time demands patience instead
Time has paused for now

Ice cream trucks went by
I thought they always would, too
Museum on wheels

Memorial Day
Fourth of July remembered
Dreaded school supplies

Midsummer embraced
June's Apostles' days
Bonfire evenings

Full bloom on Lammas
"This is My Body," He said
My heart is broken

June was forever
July was blissfully long
Difficult August

# AUTUMN

*"As long as autumn lasts, I shall not have hands, canvas and colors enough to paint the beautiful things I see."*
*— Vincent Van Gogh*

## Introduction to the original preface

Of all the introductions, this is the one which is the most difficult. For my feelings associated with the season and with my parents are vivid, still raw, and they both passed away unexpectedly. And these are the wounds—second to the loss of one's child, practically impossible to fully recuperate from. For me, I believe we do move on and ahead in life after loss—but we are never the same.

Autumn teaches us that. The season of "Fall" taught me that the inevitable death of the current year I had grown comfortable with would eventually fall, pass, and enter the realm of memory. Like the serpentine roads in New England, whose bitumen shores are overwhelmed with colors of orange, red, yellow, and brown—vivid colors that represent my vivid memories—I will wonder at as I navigate my past. But alas, they are no longer there or here with me.

The nature of the Autumnal Triduum(*Allhallowtide*) strives to impart this profound metaphysical lesson to those whose tradition includes the Triduum. This is my particular case. In essence, thin places are everywhere, but where they are most powerfully permeable is in the mind. Our consciousness is a resource where the spirit is exalted to where it should be and relegates the body to its proper place. In a world where so much is judged by the sensual and the sexual, it is refreshing and quite good to be reminded that what we take is our Self—our spirit and our consciousness—while the body is left to decay.

Only after the fullness of time is realized—and Divinity has its way with creation—will it be transformed and not be what it is today. Although it remains, it is modified to be in harmony with the spirit rather than directly contradict it as it is here on Earth. Perhaps all this is a bit too complicated for some, but I believe Allhallowtide affords us an opportunity to consider these spiritual truths.

This all made sense to me as I realized Autumn as a holy time to remember, with deep humility, we are all going to leave this place—our home—someday. I live intent on ensuring that the stone that marks my grave will have an epithet that others can share in thanksgiving for a life well lived and one that left this world slightly better as how I found it back in the Summer of '69.

My parents lived by example.

*Daniel Medina*
*July 24, 2023*
*Miami, FL*

# Preface

Autumn became my favorite season many years ago. The scents and the sights of the season made incomparable and indelible impressions in my heart and mind as a boy. I feel spiritually renewed during Autumn. Ironically, it is also a very difficult time for me as the flood of memories are unstoppable and I am overwhelmed by so many of them.

My parents' favorite season was Autumn. Perhaps this has something to do with it being mine as well. I am certain it does, of course. My mom and I would sit on the steps of our porch on late afternoons and we'd share our enthusiasm about the coming season and excitement for cooler temperatures and memorable holidays.

My first sensorial experiences associated with Autumn are associated to the cooler weather, less rain, seasonal spices—which excited my palate—and the coming festive seasons.

Writing is as much an exercise of introspection as it is an art. In the way any author or poet seeks to transmit a story, ideas, persuasive arguments, or interpretations of the human condition, so too does writing become an incomparable means of letting you, the reader, know that I am human, too.

This is the last book in the Annual Series I began at the commencement of the COVID-19 pandemic.

I made a vow to express the four seasons as I meditated upon them through Haiku. They have stood the test of time for me because poetry, like eternity, stands outside of time. My life experiences do so, too. As I mentioned at the beginning of this pilgrimage, Haiku affords anyone the opportunity to encase their deepest sense of existence and intimate experiences in words and images and yet remain anonymous. This allows the reader to use verse as a conduit to another place—towards the within—and perhaps even the divine. Nick Cave would agree. My prayer is that these poems will serve you well and be a faithful companion as you visit your own undiscovered country and return a healed *hajii.*

*Daniel Medina*
*July 10, 2021*
*Little Havana*
*Miami, FL*

# AUTUMN

## Rhythms & Recollections

We sat together
Autumn was announced by smell
From the other side

Attending school dread
Afternoons brought peace
Bullied for brilliance

*Churros y chocolate*
*El* Morro Castle
the Place
Tithes for *batidos*

Mami loved Autumn
"*Sanguiveen*" was Papi's
"*Jaloween*" for us

MOTHER.

Colors fall each day
So many beginnings, too
And I know they're gone

I'd squint to see them
Trees and sky were magical
CBS Specials

Weeding brings them out
Tokens from another time
*"Danny, que haces?"*

The All Hallows' Eve countdown
Twilight in Coral Gables
Young Goodman Brown read

Nothing exists in itself
Melville's great lesson
Ferrer's hot coffee
*Dark Side of the Moon*

Sitting there
Windows opened
Cool nights, those Fridays
Those songs changed my life

Stars continue to spy
Matching energy for them
Peak experiences

On Palm Avenue
Spoken plans for the future
Seem so long ago
Rain is coming down

Seasons were once kind
Every other weekend
I avoid seasons

Long road trips with them
Motorcycles and Zen
Lord, hear my prayer

I miss North Ashland
Part of me stayed on the porch
I am not ready

New teacher, new term
Homecoming beds on parade
Picnics on the lawn
Don't dream it's over

*La Casa de los Trucos*
Leaves change on Okeechobee
Daydreaming in French
*Voulez-vous coucher avec moi ce soir?*

Lunch in Providence
Preparing to leave it all behind
Next Thanksgiving, leave

September is near
I am reminded of death
I don't count candles

Autumn Triduum
All Saints sin, they say
As much as we pray
Gods in the making

Watching the Tropics
All pomp—some circumstances
Parents and Teachers

I made a mixtape for you
Time stopped when you walked by me
Tita and me cook
LPs with Maritere's name in ink

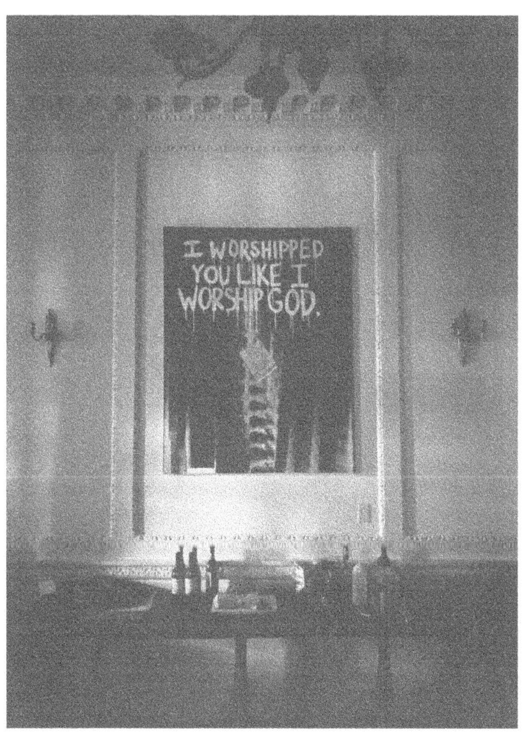

Autumn
        Some call
                        F
                            A
                                L
                                    L

Don't close the book—yet

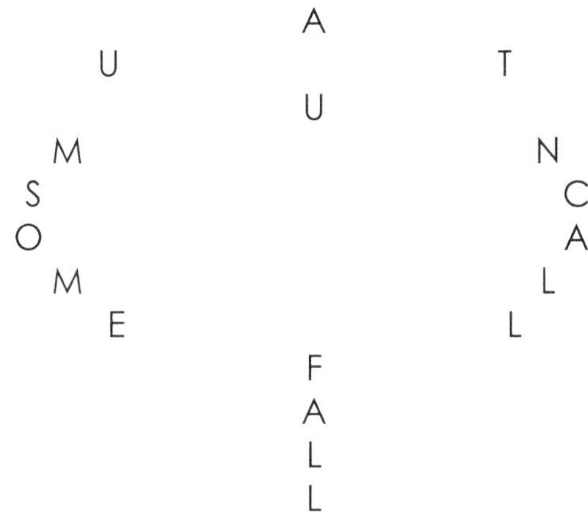


Don't close the book—yet
Four seasons at home

Really thought—
We have all the time in the world

Time won't give me time

## Acknowledgments

I would like to sincerely thank Indie Earth Publishing, and my editor Flor Ana Mireles. In an industry where so much of what is offered to the public is driven by sales, a small, independently owned, Miami-based book publishing house said, "No." Indie Earth publishes quality literature by artists who pursue their craft like a famished lion. Indie Earth seeks artists who want to share their work, inspire, question, instigate, and serve the world with the words they have been entrusted with. Thank you, Indie Earth for considering me kin. Thank you, Reader, for taking this journey through the seasons with me.

See you in
Little Havana
Go anywhere in Miami
Uber
Less stress
More stretch
Comfort

## About the Author

**Daniel Medina** was born in Chicago, Illinois, and raised in Miami, Florida. A graduate of Florida International University, Daniel went on to serve in U.S. Military Intelligence. He holds graduate degrees from the University of Oklahoma and St. Thomas University (Florida Center for Theological Studies), Miami Gardens, FL, where he earned his doctorate with distinction.

Daniel has also written and presented lectures on several topics, including Charles Williams' Theology of Romantic Love and Co-Inherence, Zen Meditation, Mindfulness, World Religions and Spirituality, Conflict Resolution, José Marti, and the American Transcendentalist Movement. Dr. Medina is a public schoolteacher and an ordained minister with the United Church of Christ. Dan is also a painter, musician, and photographer. He lives in Little Havana with his wife, Victoria.

# About the Publisher

Indie Earth Publishing Inc. is an independent, author-first co-publishing company based in Miami, FL, dedicated to giving writers the creative freedom they deserve when publishing their poetry, fiction, and short story collections. Indie Earth is a publisher for writers by a writer that provides a plethora of services meant to aid them in book publishing experiences and finally feel they are releasing the book of their dreams.

With Indie Earth Publishing, you are more than just an author, you are part of the Indie Earth creative family, making a difference one book at a time.

**www.indieearthbooks.com**

**For inquiries, please email:**
**indieearthpublishinghouse@gmail.com**

**Instagram: @indieearthbooks**

www.ingramcontent.com/pod-product-compliance
Ingram Content Group UK Ltd.
Pitfield, Milton Keynes, MK11 3LW, UK
UKHW021643190726
13853UKWH00001B/13

9 798986 210650